LLM Architectures - A Comprehensive Guide

Table of Contents: LLM Architectures - A Comprehensive Guide

- Long Short-Term Memory (LSTM) Networks

- Gated Recurrent Units (GRUs)

  o Transformers

    - Attention Mechanism

    - Encoder-Decoder Architecture

- Deep Dives into Specific Architectures:

  o BERT (Bidirectional Encoder Representations from Transformers)

    - Masked Language Modeling (MLM) for Pretraining

    - Fine-Tuning BERT for Downstream Tasks

- BART (Bidirectional and Autoregressive Transformers)
  - Leveraging Bidirectional Training for Improved Performance
  - Applications of BART in Text Generation and Summarization
- XLNet (Generalized Autoregressive Pretraining for Language Understanding)

  - Permutation Language Modeling Objective
  - Addressing Limitations of BERT with XLNet
- Comparison of Leading LLM Architectures:

- o Performance Benchmarks

- o Strengths and Weaknesses of Each Architecture

- Emerging Trends and Future Directions:

  - o Scaling LLMs to Even Greater Size

  - o Improving the Efficiency of LLM Training

  - o New LLM Architectures for Specialized Tasks (e.g., question answering, dialogue systems)

- Conclusion:

  - o The LLM Landscape - A Summary

  - o The Future of LLM Research and Development

Introduction: Demystifying Large Language Models (LLMs)

The world of artificial intelligence (AI) has witnessed a revolution in recent years, driven largely by the emergence of Large Language Models (LLMs). These sophisticated computer programs are transforming how we interact with machines and information. But what exactly are LLMs, and how did they come to be? This introduction delves into the fascinating world of

LLMs, exploring their history, applications, and the foundational architectures that make them tick.

What are Large Language Models (LLMs)?

Imagine a computer program that can not only understand human language but also generate human-quality text, translate languages, write different kinds of creative content, and answer your questions in an informative way. That's the essence of a Large Language Model. LLMs are a type of artificial intelligence trained on massive amounts of text data. This data can include books, articles, code, web pages, and even social media conversations. By analyzing these vast datasets,

LLMs learn the patterns and statistical relationships between words and sentences. This allows them to perform a variety of natural language processing (NLP) tasks, including:

- **Text Generation:** LLMs can generate different creative text formats, like poems, code, scripts, musical pieces, emails, and letters. Imagine an LLM helping a writer overcome writer's block by suggesting creative continuations for their story.

- **Machine Translation:** LLMs are revolutionizing machine translation, breaking down language barriers and enabling seamless communication across cultures.

Google Translate, for instance, utilizes LLMs to provide increasingly accurate and nuanced translations.

- **Question Answering:** LLMs can be trained on specific domains to answer your questions in an informative way. For example, a customer service LLM can answer your queries about a product or service, providing relevant information and potentially resolving your issue.

- **Text Summarization:** LLMs can condense lengthy pieces of text into concise summaries, perfect for busy professionals who need to quickly grasp the key points of an article or report.

Case Study: GPT-3 and AI Dungeon

OpenAI's GPT-3 (Generative Pre-trained Transformer 3) is a powerful LLM, known for its ability to generate realistic and creative text formats. One interesting use case is "AI Dungeon," an interactive fiction platform that utilizes GPT-3 to create unique and personalized stories for users. As you interact with the AI, it generates different narrative branches based on your choices, providing an immersive and ever-evolving storytelling experience.

A Brief History of LLMs

The concept of LLMs has its roots in the field of natural language processing (NLP) research, which has been around for decades. Early attempts involved training statistical language models on smaller datasets. However, the true turning point came with the rise of deep learning, a subfield of AI that utilizes artificial neural networks to learn complex patterns from data.

- **2013:** The introduction of recurrent neural networks (RNNs) like LSTMs (Long Short-Term Memory) marked a significant step forward. These models were able to handle longer sequences of text data compared to traditional models.

- **2017:** The release of the Transformer architecture by Google AI revolutionized the field. Transformers offered a more parallelizable and efficient approach to processing language data, leading to the development of even more powerful LLMs.

- **2018:** The emergence of pre-training techniques, where LLMs are first trained on massive datasets in an unsupervised manner, further boosted their capabilities. This pre-training allows them to be fine-tuned for specific NLP tasks, demonstrating impressive performance gains.

Today, LLMs continue to evolve at a rapid pace, with researchers pushing the boundaries of their capabilities and exploring new applications across various industries.

Applications of LLMs: Transforming Industries

The potential applications of LLMs are vast and constantly expanding. Here are some key areas where LLMs are making a significant impact:

- **Customer Service:** LLMs can power chatbots that can answer customer queries, troubleshoot problems, and even personalize interactions.

- **Content Creation:** LLMs can assist writers and content creators by generating ideas, outlines, and even drafts of content, streamlining the content creation process.

- **Education:** LLMs can be used to develop personalized learning experiences, provide feedback on student writing, and even act as virtual tutors.

- **Healthcare:** LLMs can analyze medical records to identify potential health risks, translate medical documents, and even generate reports.

- **Legal Services:** LLMs can be used to analyze legal documents, conduct research, and even help with drafting legal contracts.

Example: Using LLMs for Drug Discovery

In the field of medicine, researchers are exploring the use of LLMs to accelerate drug discovery. By analyzing vast amounts of scientific literature and medical data, LLMs can help identify potential drug targets and generate new drug candidates. This has the potential to significantly reduce the

Foundational Architectures for LLMs: Building the Blocks of Language Understanding

While LLMs seem like magic, their capabilities are built upon powerful neural network architectures. These architectures are essentially the building blocks that allow LLMs to learn and process language. Here, we'll delve into two key foundational architectures that have paved the way for modern LLMs:

Recurrent Neural Networks (RNNs): Capturing Context in Sequences

Imagine a conversation. To understand the meaning of a current sentence, you need to consider what was said before. Similarly, LLMs need a way to capture the context of sequential data, like sentences in a paragraph. This is where Recurrent Neural Networks (RNNs) come into play. RNNs are a type of neural network specifically designed to handle sequential data.

Here's the core idea: An RNN takes an input, processes it through a hidden layer, and then combines the output of that layer with the current input to create a new hidden state. This hidden state essentially acts as a "memory" that allows the network to consider past information when processing the current input. This process is repeated for each element in the sequence, enabling the RNN to learn the relationships between words within a sentence or document.

However, RNNs have limitations. One challenge is the vanishing gradient problem. In RNNs with long sequences, the influence of earlier inputs can fade away as the network processes information further down the sequence. This makes it difficult for the network to learn long-term dependencies within the data.

Long Short-Term Memory (LSTM) Networks: Overcoming the Limitations of RNNs

To address the limitations of RNNs, a special type of RNN called a Long Short-Term Memory (LSTM) network was developed. LSTMs incorporate a special "cell" structure that allows them to selectively remember or forget information over time. This cell contains gates that control the flow of information:

- **Input Gate:** Decides which new information to store in the cell's memory.
- **Forget Gate:** Decides what information to forget from the cell's current memory.

- **Output Gate:** Determines what information from the cell's memory to include in the output.

With these gates, LSTMs can effectively learn long-term dependencies within sequential data, making them a powerful tool for tasks like machine translation and speech recognition.

Use Case: Using LSTMs for Stock Price Prediction

LSTMs can be used in finance to analyze historical stock price data and predict future trends. By considering past price movements, trading volumes, and other relevant factors, LSTMs can learn complex patterns and identify potential market signals. It's important to note that these predictions are not guarantees, but LSTMs can be a valuable tool for financial analysts.

Gated Recurrent Units (GRUs): A Simpler Alternative to LSTMs

Gated Recurrent Units (GRUs) are another variant of RNNs that address the vanishing gradient problem. Similar to LSTMs, they use gates to control the flow of information. However, GRUs have a simpler architecture compared to LSTMs, making them computationally more efficient. While generally less powerful than LSTMs, GRUs can be a good choice for tasks where computational efficiency is a priority.

These foundational architectures, RNNs, LSTMs, and GRUs, have laid the groundwork for the development of more sophisticated architectures like transformers, which we will explore in the next section. By understanding these building blocks, we gain a deeper appreciation for the complexities involved in building powerful LLMs.

Deep Dives into Specific Architectures: Unveiling the Powerhouse Techniques

Having explored the foundational architectures of RNNs, LSTMs, and GRUs, we now delve deeper into the world of cutting-edge LLM architectures. Here, we'll take a magnifying glass to three specific models that have revolutionized the field: BERT, BART, and XLNet.

BERT (Bidirectional Encoder Representations from Transformers): A Revolution in Pre-training

BERT (Bidirectional Encoder Representations from Transformers) stands as a landmark achievement in the field of LLMs. Introduced by Google AI in 2018, BERT ushered in a new era of pre-training techniques, significantly boosting the capabilities of LLMs.

Understanding Transformers: The Engine Behind BERT

Before diving into BERT itself, let's shed light on the transformer architecture, the engine that powers its success. Transformers are a neural network architecture specifically designed for sequence-to-sequence tasks, like machine translation and text summarization. Unlike RNNs, which process data sequentially, transformers can analyze all elements of a sequence simultaneously, making them much faster and more efficient.

At the heart of the transformer lies the **attention mechanism**. This mechanism allows the model to focus on specific parts of the input sequence that are most relevant to the current element being processed. Imagine reading a sentence. The attention mechanism lets the model pay closer attention to words that are crucial for understanding the meaning, similar to how you might focus on key phrases while reading a complex paragraph.

Masked Language Modeling (MLM): The Secret Sauce of BERT's Pre-training

One of BERT's key innovations lies in its pre-training technique called Masked Language Modeling (MLM). Here's how it works:

1. **Masking:** Random words in a sentence are replaced with a special "[MASK]" token.

2. **Prediction:** The model then tries to predict the original masked words based on the surrounding context.

This process forces BERT to learn deep contextual relationships between words, effectively teaching it the intricacies of language. It's like playing a game of fill-in-the-blank, but on a massive scale with real text data.

Case Study: Fine-Tuning BERT for Sentiment Analysis

BERT's power lies in its pre-trained capabilities. Imagine you train a chef on a vast array of cuisines (pre-training). This chef can then apply their knowledge to create new dishes specific to a particular region (fine-tuning). Similarly, a pre-trained BERT model can be fine-tuned for various downstream tasks.

For instance, let's say you want to build a system that can analyze customer reviews and determine if they are positive, negative, or neutral (sentiment analysis). You can take a pre-trained BERT model and fine-tune it on a labeled dataset of customer reviews with sentiment labels. This fine-tuning process adds an additional output layer to the model, allowing it to classify reviews based on the sentiment it has learned to identify.

Next Steps: Exploring BART and XLNet

BERT has paved the way for further advancements in LLM architectures. In the following sections, we'll delve into two exciting architectures that build upon the foundation laid by BERT: BART (Bidirectional and Autoregressive Transformers) and XLNet (Generalized Autoregressive Pretraining for Language Understanding). These models introduce new approaches to pre-training and

tackle some of the limitations of BERT, further

pushing the boundaries of what LLMs can achieve.

BART (Bidirectional and Autoregressive Transformers): Going Beyond Masked Language Modeling

BART (Bidirectional and Autoregressive Transformers), introduced in 2018 by researchers at Facebook, represents another significant leap forward in LLM architectures. Building upon the success of BERT, BART offers several key improvements, particularly in the area of text generation tasks.

Leveraging Bidirectional Training for Improved Performance

One of the key differences between BERT and

BART lies in their pre-training strategies. While

BERT relies on Masked Language Modeling (MLM),

BART utilizes a technique called **denoising

autoencoding**. Here's how it works:

1. **Input Corruption:** The model is given a

   sentence where a portion of the text is

   replaced with noise (e.g., random characters).

2. **Reconstruction:** The model then attempts to

   reconstruct the original, noise-free sentence.

This process allows BART to learn not only from

the masked elements but also from the

surrounding context in a bidirectional manner,

similar to how humans read and understand

language. This

This process allows BART to learn not only from

the masked elements but also from the

surrounding context in a bidirectional manner,

similar to how humans read and understand

language. This bidirectional training approach is

believed to contribute to BART's superior

performance in tasks like text generation and

summarization.

Applications of BART in Text Generation and

Summarization

BART's ability to effectively capture contextual relationships makes it a powerful tool for various text generation tasks. Here are some examples:

- **Creative Text Writing:** Imagine needing help brainstorming ideas for a story or poem. BART can be fine-tuned to generate different creative text formats, providing prompts and inspiration to overcome writer's block.

- **Machine Translation:** BART demonstrates strong performance in machine translation tasks. Its ability to understand the nuances of language in both the source and target languages allows for more accurate and natural-sounding translations.

- **Dialogue Systems:** BART can be fine-tuned to create chatbots that can engage in more natural and coherent conversations with users. By considering the entire conversation history, BART can generate more relevant and informative responses.

Case Study: Using BART for Automatic News Summarization

News outlets are constantly bombarded with information. BART can be a valuable tool for automatically generating concise summaries of news articles. Imagine a busy professional who needs to quickly grasp the key points of several news articles. A BART-based summarization system can analyze these articles and provide summaries that highlight the most important information, saving time and effort.

Beyond text generation, BART also excels in tasks like text summarization. Its ability to condense lengthy pieces of text while preserving the core meaning makes it ideal for applications where information overload is a challenge.

Exploring XLNet

While BART offers significant advantages, it's not

the only contender in the LLM architecture race. In

the next section, we'll explore XLNet (Generalized

Autoregressive Pretraining for Language

Understanding), another powerful architecture that tackles some of the limitations of BERT and presents a unique approach to pre-training.

Deep Dives into Specific Architectures

XLNet (Generalized Autoregressive Pretraining for Language Understanding): Addressing Limitations and Exploring New Frontiers

XLNet, introduced by researchers at Google AI in 2019, stands as another groundbreaking LLM architecture. Building upon the success of BERT, XLNet addresses some of its limitations and introduces a novel pre-training objective called the Permutation Language Modeling (PLM) objective.

Permutation Language Modeling Objective: A More Comprehensive Approach

One of the shortcomings of BERT's Masked Language Modeling (MLM) is that it only considers masked elements in a single, fixed context. XLNet tackles this by introducing the Permutation Language Modeling (PLM) objective. Here's the core idea:

- **Permutation:** The model is given a sentence where the order of the words is shuffled randomly.

- **Reconstruction:** The model then attempts to predict the original, correctly ordered sentence based on the shuffled version.

This process forces XLNet to consider all possible word orders and their relationships within a sentence. This is analogous to how humans can understand the meaning of a sentence even if the words are jumbled up to a certain extent. The model essentially learns to "de-scramble" the sentence and reconstruct the intended meaning.

Addressing Limitations of BERT with XLNet

The PLM objective offers several advantages over MLM:

- **Tackling Bidirectionality:** Unlike MLM, which is unidirectional (predicting masked words based on the left context), PLM considers all possible word orders, effectively capturing bidirectional relationships between words.

- **Mitigating Pre-training Bottleneck:** MLM can sometimes struggle with longer sequences due to vanishing gradients. PLM, by considering all permutations, avoids this issue and can effectively handle longer sequences.

Beyond Reconstruction: Leveraging Autoregressive Modeling

While reconstruction is a core component of PLM, XLNet also incorporates **autoregressive modeling**. This means the model predicts each word in the sentence based on the previous words it has already generated. This allows XLNet to not only reconstruct existing sentences but also generate entirely new ones, similar to how humans naturally produce language one word at a time.

The Road Ahead: Exploring the Potential of LLMs

With advancements like BERT, BART, and XLNet, the field of LLMs is rapidly evolving. These architectures are pushing the boundaries of what's possible in terms of natural language processing.

As we continue to explore and refine these models,

we can expect even more exciting developments in

the years to come, opening doors to new

applications and transforming the way we interact

with technology and information.

Comparison of Leading LLM Architectures:

Unveiling the Champions

Having explored the intricacies of BERT, BART, and XLNet, we now enter the arena of comparison. These architectures, while sharing some core functionalities, possess distinct strengths and weaknesses that make them suitable for different tasks. This section delves into a head-to-head comparison, analyzing their performance on benchmarks, highlighting their strengths, and uncovering their limitations.

Performance Benchmarks: Putting the LLMs to the Test

Evaluating LLM performance is a complex endeavor, as it depends heavily on the specific task and dataset used. However, certain benchmarks have emerged as standard tools for comparing different architectures. Here, we'll focus on two key benchmarks:

- **GLUE (General Language Understanding Evaluation):** This benchmark suite assesses an LLM's performance on various natural language processing tasks like question answering, sentiment analysis, and natural language inference.

- **SQuAD (Stanford Question Answering Dataset):** This benchmark specifically focuses on an LLM's ability to answer questions posed on a set of reading comprehension passages.

Case Study: Comparing LLM Performance on GLUE

A 2020 study by researchers at Google AI compared the performance of BERT, BART, and XLNet on the GLUE benchmark suite. The results revealed some interesting insights:

- **BERT:** Achieved strong performance on most tasks, demonstrating its versatility. However, it struggled slightly on tasks requiring reasoning or commonsense knowledge.

- **BART:** Outperformed both BERT and XLNet on tasks like natural language inference and sentiment analysis. This highlights its ability to capture subtle nuances in language.

- **XLNet:** Showcased competitive performance on most tasks, particularly excelling in question answering based on the SQuAD dataset.

It's important to remember that these are just a few examples, and the optimal LLM for a specific task will depend on various factors.

Strengths and Weaknesses of Each Architecture: A Closer Look

Now that we've explored some performance benchmarks, let's delve deeper into the strengths and weaknesses of each architecture:

BERT:

Strengths:

- **Versatility:** Performs well on a wide range of NLP tasks.

- **Efficiency:** Relatively computationally efficient compared to other architectures.

- **Availability:** Widely available pre-trained models and easy-to-use fine-tuning methods.

Weaknesses:

- **Unidirectional Training:** Limited ability to capture bidirectional relationships between words.

- **Masking Strategy:** Masking only a portion of the input can limit the model's understanding of context.

BART:

Strengths:

- **Bidirectional Training:** Effectively captures context through its denoising autoencoding approach.

- **Text Generation:** Excels in tasks like text summarization and creative text writing due to its ability to generate coherent sequences.

- **Strong Language Understanding:** Demonstrates excellent performance on tasks requiring nuanced understanding of language.

Weaknesses:

- **Computational Cost:** Training BART can be computationally more expensive compared to BERT.

- **Fine-Tuning Complexity:** Fine-tuning BART for specific tasks can be more challenging compared to BERT.

XLNet:

Strengths:

- **Comprehensive Pre-training:** The PLM objective allows XLNet to consider all possible word orders and relationships, leading to a deeper understanding of language.

- **Handling Long Sequences:** Effectively tackles longer sequences due to its ability to avoid vanishing gradients.

- **Question Answering:** Shows exceptional performance on question answering tasks due to its ability to reason and identify key information within context.

Weaknesses:

- **Training Complexity:** Training XLNet can be even more computationally expensive compared to BART.

- **Interpretability:** The inner workings of XLNet can be more complex to understand compared to other architectures, making it challenging to debug or analyze model behavior.

Choosing the Right LLM: It's All About the Task

There's no single "best" LLM architecture. The optimal choice depends on the specific task at hand. Consider these factors when selecting an LLM:

- **Task Requirements:** Does the task require strong text generation capabilities, comprehensive language understanding, or exceptional question answering abilities?

- **Computational Resources:** Do you have access to the necessary computational power to train and fine-tune the LLM?

- **Available Expertise:** Do you have the expertise required to work with potentially more complex architectures like XLNet?

By understanding the strengths and weaknesses of each architecture, you can make an informed decision and leverage the power of LLMs to achieve your specific goals.

Emerging Trends and Future Directions: Pushing the Boundaries of LLMs

The world of LLMs is a dynamic landscape, constantly evolving and pushing the boundaries of what's possible. In this section, we'll explore some of the most exciting emerging trends and future directions in LLM research and development.

Scaling LLMs to Even Greater Size: The Quest for More Power

One of the defining trends in LLM research is the quest for ever-larger models. The rationale behind this is simple: larger models have the potential to learn more complex relationships between words and concepts, leading to improved performance on various tasks.

Case Study: The Rise of Megatron-Turing NLG

In 2022, Google AI and NVIDIA unveiled Megatron-Turing NLG, a colossal LLM with a staggering 530 billion parameters. This model demonstrated significant improvements on various benchmarks, showcasing the potential benefits of scaling. For instance, it achieved state-of-the-art performance on tasks like question answering and summarization.

However, scaling LLMs comes with challenges:

- **Computational Cost:** Training and running these massive models requires immense computational resources, making them expensive and energy-consuming.

- **Data Bottleneck:** Feeding these models with enough high-quality data to train them effectively is a significant challenge.

- **Interpretability:** As models grow larger, it becomes increasingly difficult to understand their inner workings and decision-making processes.

Researchers are actively exploring ways to mitigate these challenges, such as developing more efficient training algorithms, utilizing specialized hardware architectures, and employing data augmentation techniques to create more training data.

Improving the Efficiency of LLM Training: Doing More with Less

While scaling offers immense potential, there's a growing emphasis on improving the efficiency of LLM training. This involves finding ways to train powerful LLMs with fewer resources and data.

Example: Knowledge Distillation for Efficient LLM Training

Knowledge distillation is a technique where a smaller, more efficient model learns from a larger, pre-trained model. The larger model acts as a "teacher," and the smaller model acts as a "student." Through this process, the student model can learn the essential knowledge from the teacher without requiring the same amount of training data or computational resources.

Here are some other strategies for improving training efficiency:

- **Transfer Learning:** Leveraging pre-trained models for specific tasks instead of training from scratch.

- **Curriculum Learning:** Gradually increasing the difficulty of training data as the model learns, allowing it to focus on areas where it needs improvement.

- **Pruning and Quantization:** Techniques for reducing the number of parameters in a model and making them more efficient to store and compute.

By employing these methods, researchers aim to democratize access to LLMs, making them more accessible for a wider range of applications and users.

Next Steps: Exploring New Architectures for Specialized Tasks

While large, general-purpose LLMs are impressive, there's a growing interest in developing specialized LLM architectures for specific tasks. In the following section, we'll delve into this exciting area of research.

www.ingramcontent.com/pod-product-compliance
Lightning Source LLC
LaVergne TN
LVHW051617050326
832903LV00033B/4537